Spiritual Journey of
AIKIDO

HUW DILLON

Paul H. Crompton Ltd.
94 Felsham Road
London SW15 1DQ

First Edition 1997
© Huw Dillon 1996
ISBN No 1 874250 35 9

All rights reserved. No part of this system may be reproduced, stored in a retrieval system or transmitted in any form or by any means electronic, mechanical, photocopying, recording or otherwise without prior permission of the publishers.

London: Paul H.Crompton Ltd.
94 Felsham Road, Putney, London SW15 1DQ

New York: Talman Company
131 Spring Street, New York, N.Y. 10012, U.S.A.

*Printed and bound in England
by Caric Press
Clerwood, Corunna Main,
Andover, Hants SP10 1JE
(01264) 354887*

ACKNOWLEDGEMENTS

I wish to thank my uke Alan Taylor and photographer Stuart Robinson.

Especially thanks to my Sensei Jan, who introduced me to Aikido.

Also I wish to mention and thank the Reiyukai Oriental Arts Centre, Norwich for the use of its facilities.

*"I did not create Aikido.
Aiki is the wisdom of God.
Aikido is the Way of the Laws which He created".*

Morihei Ueshiba, Founder of Aikido

Contents

Introduction 3
Your Path as Uke 6
Harmony 9
Aikido Teaching 10
Techniques 11
Locks 16
Hands & Bow 18
Aikido Training 19
Yoga, Tai Chi,, Aikido 21
Beginners 23
Attacks 25
Techa Nage 62
Using Tegatana 70
Using Finger & Thumb 80
Use of Ki 84
Conclusion 86

INTRODUCTION

Aikido training is about love. It is one of the ways to strip away the self. The heavy armour that one calls oneself, and to reveal the being that reflects the love of the universe.

Aikido training is purely spiritual. It is not a martial art. It is not a self defence system. It is a spiritual way, the self defence is merely part of it. The self defence system and the martial does cause people to become stuck in the wrong system. Other items such as gradings and coloured belts, distract from the correct path. They produce conflict in the form of competition. How can you grade a person's spiritual state?

The beginners spiritual state may far exceed long term practitioners. You can not grade, it is ridiculous to try. It is a mockery of what you are trying to achieve, which is to free oneself of the world.

To grow through Aikido training, first you must wish to do this, secondly you must be prepared to be totally honest, and admit all faults to yourself, regardless of whether they are seen by others or not. You can not lie to yourself, if you do, or if you make excuses for your actions, you will not grow. Aikido training does not, and should not just go on in the dojo. It is a way of life, the awareness you begin to perceive on the mat must also be nurtured off the mat. I mean really nurtured.

Many practitioners tip out platitudes of Aikido truths and practices which they do not understand, cannot understand, will not understand, because their ego is too strong. Yes, we come to the ego. The ego is the personality, the clutter, the armour we build around ourselves. Yes, this is the part to be totally destroyed. There is only one way to deal with the ego, and that is complete ruthlessness. It must be ripped out. Then the sun will shine, and love will flood the being. This is enlightenment, union with God. This may seem far beyond you, but it is not. It is the only aim that every man, woman, and child should ever want to achieve. It is our reason for living.

Much Aikido is taught by Sensei who do not question what they teach. They just pass on the teachings and techniques they have learnt. Nothing wrong with this you might say, but there is. It is not alive. It is not an alive teaching. It is dead, because it is not taught with authority and understanding. This can only be done by one who knows and understands the true nature of Aikido, and teaches it that way. Just passing on information is equivalent to an exam syllabus, there is no heart. The sensei must love, be consumed by Aikido, and his love for the art will touch and kindle some of his students. Not many are prepared to take this road. It takes courage, for your training will raise deep penetrating soul searching questions, which you must be prepared to answer before you pass on. I have seen many funk and leave when this stage is reached. This can be after several years, but usually within the first year. Or others stay on the same level, refusing to look beyond. Others go and train with a same sensei, one who just passes on information. All this because the ego is threatened . This horrible mass of human experience which does not want to be destroyed, and so will protect itself with many laudable and plausible excuses, but all are rubbish to be forced aside by the serious student.

Aikido, what is it? It is the study of energy, Ki energy, life energy. We learn our relationship to this energy, through training with a partner or partners. Every movement and thought is energy. We learn to feel this energy as we wake our bodies up. Most peoples bodies and their consciousness are asleep, and stay completely asleep until they die. Aikido will jolt that sleep if you will allow. A note of warning, this energy can be used correctly for love and spiritual growth, or incorrectly for power, greed, domination over others. It is a choice that you will face at a certain time, if you seriously train. If you have trained correctly, you can only possibly choose the right way. Once you begin to see and understand this energy, you will understand its misuse. In the form of the black arts, for it is all the same root.

The movements and techniques of Aikido are vehicles for teaching the body how to move. They are important, and yet unimportant. No training is wasted, but if you wish to grow from the martial, then you must change emphasis, and remember softness. Softness is not weakness, it is softness, and stronger than strength, for as it is soft, it does not shatter. As you train, you must become as the grass that sways before the wind. It does not break. This is how you must move, when in the path of your uke's energy. Allow your partner's energy to blow you aside, feel it, then disappear.

YOUR PATH AS AN UKE

In training, the movement between partners is one. It starts with the first movement of your uke, and finishes with the end of the throw. We must not separate ourselves into attacker and attacked. We are learning about energy and movement, not domination. Aikido should have its martial tag removed, practiced in its true spirit it is not martial. It is the art, and I stress the word art, of love and harmony. We must learn to train in total trust, then we can grow. Aikido is a spiritual journey and must permeate your entire life and being.

The art of Aikido is to move with a completeness, taking the strongest fastest movement your partner makes. You must flow with the movement, you must train hard to remove the slap of hands and wrists meeting, it should be a soundless meeting. A gentle taking of your partners Ki, even though it maybe at great speed. You must also protect your partner from injury at all times. You are learning about energy, you must be aware of your partner's weight, size, speed, balance. Ki, everything. This awareness carries from partner to partner, but it has to be worked very hard for. Never force any movement, especially if it might injure your partner. If you are wrong, let the movement go. Start again and feel your way through. Remember softness is the way of Aikido. Aikido taught otherwise is not true Aikido. Softness is not weakness, just softness, and it is difficult to attain, work at it. Remember as your uke's strike comes in, that you are not there, you disappear. You completely yield to the touch, yet you leave your touch for your partner to contact. He struggles to hold that contact, you must leave it there, so that it is real, yet melts away, leaving your partner falling, lost in movement.

The uke's position must be completely understood, and everyone must become a good uke if they wish to grow. Training is a very special training. In one sense it is very artificial, for one trains against a set movement with a set consequence. The uke must completely understand each movement, for if not, you do not give the opportunity for your partner to move correctly. For each technique is a lesson, a fragment in a particular type of energy and if the uke misinterprets it, then the lesson is lost. A good uke must trust, but this must always be mutual. He must allow full use of his body and give it generously. Anybody who misuses or abuses this trust does not understand Aikido training. Gentleness must always be the path. Of course there are always the accidents that happen, but they are not from anger or frustration, but from not moving fast enough or too soon. Without a good uke it is very difficult to learn and progress in Aikido, so help each other. You can learn from a difficult uke, for they will teach you other ways of dealing with unexpected energy, especially if you understand their unhelpful movements.

A Sensei has problems with wrongly moving ukes, they do not understand what is required of them. If the energy is not correct the Sensei cannot demonstrate the movement he wishes to. He can do something else with that energy, for the energy dictates the movement. A Sensei will correct an uke if his movement and energy is wrong. He will explain why it is wrong, and demonstrate the correct movement and energy. Every situation is a chance to teach and explain. We can learn much from these situations, grab them, do not just dismiss them as having gone wrong.

There is a great depth to Aikido. As you understand this, so you will discover what I call the big grin. The great sense of humour that will emerge as you train. You will have found it, if you laugh heartily when you are hit, especially on the face or head, which must happen occasionally, assuming it's not too hard a blow.

Aikido is full contact, it hurts if you do not get out of the way. Through each movement you are touching your partner's body down one side, or if not touching, just allowing a very small gap between you. Do not force your partners body around you, watch the energy, make a gate and step through. Allow your partner's energy its passage, then direct it so that there is no chance of your partner pulling out or countering your movement. This is when you are really beginning to flow. Your partner should experience nothing until he lands on the mat. No jerks or slams, just a complete absence of anything, except the whirl of energy. And it should be a whirl of energy, your uke should not know what has happened, even if he knows the technique.

As you train you must learn to lighten your body. This protects your body and increases your flow. Many people in the early stages have a muscle orientated movement, this is the part to leave behind. This can only be achieved by regular training and it will allow you to become a good uke. Once a good uke, then you begin to understand Aikido.

HARMONY

Listen very carefully to this. This is how you must understand completely Aikido, and what is required of you. Harmony, that word, look at it and find its depth. For when you train and take your partner's energy from a blow or kick, you bring him into harmony if you are training correctly. To bring your partner into harmony, you must be in harmony. Not wishing to hurt, to dominate or inflicting yourself onto your partner. You must be in harmony, love, divine love. Now look further. As you come to understand the bringing into harmony of your partner, should you not bring other things into harmony in your daily life. As you move in harmony so you will cause other situations to come into harmony. This is where your Aikido training really comes into your everyday life, and it must. You do not have to wait until a high level is achieved before it happens. It begins immediately you start serious correct training.

AIKIDO TEACHING

Practitioners can travel from one Aikido dojo to another and recognise the training, and feel reasonably at home in each. This should not be, there should be art taught in each dojo. Of course they would recognise the essential elements of harmony and known techniques, but beyond this each sensei should be teaching his own art of understanding Aikido. If not, he needs to seriously continue training until he opens, allowing his own art to form. I do teach known techniques, but mostly I teach techniques and movements that confuse and cause students to search. I use energy, movement and Ki in many unexpected ways to achieve this. This causes growth by understanding, swelling their awareness. Much Aikido training is flat, one dimensional. I teach a multi-dimensional discipline. As you train you must search and seek out all that is hidden in each movement taught. The more you progress, the more you will find, and only you can do this work.

I believe every martial art should have its martial tag removed, for they are all spiritual disciplines first. Retaining the martial tag is an excuse for violence and retaining violence. Violence is not part of any spiritual discipline. There is no more room in this world for warriors in the martial way. There is only room for warriors of the self, those who will continue to struggle through every layer of the ego until it is left behind. This path of Aikido will help if it is your path. One day you will look back along your path of struggle, and say to yourself, "It is simple, but oh so hard to know so". Then you again turn and struggle on, for it is never over, you never rest. You must ever be vigilant to keep growing, it is very easy to stagnate.

TECHNIQUES

I have demonstrated several techniques within this book which may seem simple, are simple, but have a great depth. At one level students may think they have the movement, but to really discover the movement you must sink into it completely and understand its energy completely, and that is the difficult part.

I have incorporated photographs taken on a slow shutter speed. They demonstrate how both become one movement, and that you cannot possibly move separately from your uke. Also you can see how the uke moves around your centre as he is taken and thrown. Other photographs demonstrate the movements which I refer to as the trailing arm techniques. These require a movement of the body away from the uke, but leaving an arm behind which floats with the energy of the cut or punch. When the cut or punch is exhausted the arm continues its circle, which takes the uke into a throw. These movements are designed to educate each in unusual movements, which will eventually lead to free movement.

I do not write to teach new techniques, but to inspire and awaken a searching for spiritual growth through training. To make you realise if your training is stuck and not living. Your training should uplift you and make your whole body vibrant as you step onto the mat and off it.

There is a point you will reach where you will begin to have insights into your training. Eventually you will begin to teach yourself through training. The training teaches you and guides you, listen. You must be aware to feel and know this. Do not become arrogant or complacent, for then you will lose this gift, many never find it.

A. A beautiful example of blending together. It shows well the centre of the movement which the uke spins around.

B. The lining up of centre to the circle of the arm and the positioning of the hips. This is just before the throw. Notice the close position of body contact.

C. The power of the throw about to be released

D. The blending of movement. Notice how the uke's centre is swept away.

E. The throw in progress. Full power just being unleashed.

F. Circle forming with the uke moving around the centre.

G. Notice the power and strength, even though it is soft within the movement.

H. The complete circle. Notice the soft release of the uke.

LOCKS

I have said Aikido is not to be treated as a martial art, and that is so, but it does not mean that you can be sloppy. It requires an internal discipline far more rigorous than anyone external can apply. You finish the movements, you make sure you face your uke as you throw and he lands. You make sure that if he springs up that you are ready. That as you throw you make sure you are not caught by flying feet or an elbow or knee. You must be aware at all times. You must make sure that the arm lock is applied correctly, and that as you leave your partner you watch him as you move away, Every small detail must be noted. When using wrist locks, arm locks, none should ever be slammed on. They are fast, but gently applied. Just a gentle use of nikkyo will drop your partner to the mat. You do not need to mangle his wrist all the way to the mat. You must develop a sensitive use of locks, then they will work well and will not damage anybody. As you feel your way into the locks, so you will feel your way into every movement. You will feel your way into your partner's centre, and every time you will feel the control of the centre and movement of the centre. The centre is not your possession, it is a movement of energy to blend with, not to be exploited, possessed or dominated. It is free, and as you understand this you will also become free. One can read many words on Aikido, but there is no substitute for training get on the mat. Do not make excuses for missing sessions, one can always find a plausible excuse. Be particular where you train, check the sensei out. See if it is the way you wish to train. If not, find another. Wrong direction is to be avoided.

As you move your body it must be strongly rooted to the ground, totally in balance, but able to move anywhere.

The balance comes from the centre, the tanden point, feel it, move from it. Be aware of using strength, just forget it. Your muscles should be relaxed. You do not need to tense at any time, it will block your energy and movement. Learn to flow, and that is hard, but it is the only way and far stronger than any use of muscle. Use of muscle is very ego orientated . It is using force to dominate, not seeking to blend and disappear. When beginning training, learning to leave the crude muscle strength out of the movements is difficult. As one progresses it has to be always watched and admitted to. You must be honest and never fear looking a fool, that is the ego talking. Just get stuck in and train. Please remember moving fast is not flowing, it is just moving fast, you must bond with your partner, you must become one movement to flow.

HANDS

As you train become aware of your hands. Many people just spray the fingers out and push through like paddles. The hand is alive as is the arm and the rest of the body. But alive, that is it can feel, hear and see. It snakes, pivots around wrists, cuts, places holds with incredible precision. Feel the Ki, feel your life energy pouring through. If your hands do not feel like this, then you have an energy block. Try to allow the energy to flow. Start by being aware of your hands as you train, you will feel the difference. Remember always when moving around your ukes wrists, never to close the grip for this stops your movement and blocks your energy. You can hold with the curve of the hand using the little finger as you move your partner, or in the open vee of finger and thumb. Sometimes you might close air and fire fingers to thumb, but never close all four fingers and thumb in a clenched grip. It is hard, and as I have said blocks your energy. Keep fluid even when pinning somebody down in an arm lock, you may need to rise.

THE BOW

As we bow, we bare the back of our necks to each other. A bow of mutual trust. There are no points to win, no battles to play, you are open, open to all, no protection, naked, and naked you grow.

AIKIDO TRAINING

When I train and teach I move so that I have become the movement. I feel for balance, always searching for weakness in my movements, always aware of my uke. I do not teach Aikido as a martial art, but I do teach it to be exact, controlled, aware and flowing. There must be a reason for every move, no unnecessary movements. So when watched by an outsider, it looks totally martial, but isn't. To the initiated who can follow the flow, the feel and laughter, it is different to a martial class. People do not smile or laugh when training the martial way.

Arm locks and wrist locks are just applied enough to drop or arrest your partner. There is no reason to cause pain by wrenching wrists and arms. It should be over in a moment with your partner in the required position. Any unnecessary time spent on locks stops you from moving, so producing an energy block. Your energy should just flow everywhere, do not block it by hard grips. The great rule is to become simple in movement. Watch a beginner struggling with a technique, and the amount of strength and energy they put into it. You can see what they are doing wrong, you tell them to relax their shoulders, put their arms in the correct position and explain why. Each has to learn how to be simple and that is deep and difficult.

There are levels of consciousness in training and life. Unless you are aware of these levels, in fact have moved through several levels, you will not know of their existence. When you train you may have to drop levels. Be aware of it, remember you had to travel up and that your partner is on the same path, help him or her.

Many move in straight lines, search for the curve for every movement is curved. If you hurt your partner, it is probably because you have left the curve out. Always move the curve from or to your centre co-ordinated with correct breathing. When moving your partner, feel, be aware of their body, don't thrust it around like a gate. Move with the body, feel its limitations, its circles, its softness. Do not forget that you are trying to wake up your consciousness. Becoming aware of your partner will allow you to know how to move them, it will reveal the flow.

Never think that you have got to the top or that you are superior, you are not, this is especially dangerous in graded situations. As for reaching the top, there isn't a top. There is an opening which grows constantly as our consciousness grows, there are no boundaries. Correct growth through the discipline of Aikido will produce a complete human being. On your journey you will encounter the many levels of anger, fear, jealousy, hate, which peel away as you work at them. There is a point where you can leave them all behind. Where you will see them arise, but where you can leave them and not be bound to them, you must wish to do this. I know that I am talking about a depth of growth that few even know about, especially when we first begin to train in Aikido. If we listen and open it becomes an unescapable journey which spreads from the mat into every facet of our lives, but we must be prepared to make a commitment far beyond just regular training.

THE CONNECTIONS OF YOGA, TAI CHI AND AIKIDO

Pay attention to your breathing, learn to breathe in as you build your Ki, and breathe out as you release your Ki such as when throwing. As you learn techniques make sure you understand the breathing of the movements, for it will help you to flow and use less energy. The further we progress the less we have to move. Remember to breathe to the tanden point, the centre of the abdomen. Breathe in through your nose and out through your mouth. Correct breathing strengthens the body. Many of the Aikido warming up exercises come from Yoga and all should incorporate correct breathing. Yoga training complements Aikido training, it will heal and strengthen your body, also the training of breathing will change your Aikido.

As you progress you will understand the common core of all the arts. You will understand their energies and how they should be practiced, and how often they are not practiced correctly. Judo long ago left the spiritual path and also many forms of Karate. Tai Chi is one of the few that follows a spiritual path, but quite often it is wrongly taught. Many just teach dead energy, and it just stays in that limited form. Tai Chi like all arts has to be broken out of, and one has to be brave to do it. All taught sequences must be understood, and then left behind as you travel on understanding more of Ki energy and the universe. Tai Chi carries the same spiritual path as Aikido, they are both the same. Tai Chi movements come freely without learning any taught patterns for the Aikido practitioner who has left behind technique, and who is creating his art and exploring the universe. Here he has begun to break into real freedom and understanding. These areas are open to all who strive, but it can't possibly be owned or graded. These Tai Chi movements that come are the soft and delicate movements of Aikido at a deep level. The practitioner understands these movements, but does not own them. He can teach them and students can copy the movements, but they will not have the understanding of their depth unless they are nearing a deep level themselves. This does not mean that you should give up, it means training, searching, looking and understanding, gradually the secrets will be revealed.

Thoughts are energy and thoughts are concrete. You will find that as you train you will become partners thoughts and movements. You will often read his or her movements and thoughts. This is your consciousness expanding, think of the beginner, you can read their thoughts and movements. You register their alarm when they see flying breakfalls from throws, or the speed with which an attack comes. You tell them it's not difficult and that with time they will be able to do the same, and that they aren't expected to do that just yet. Well even long standing practitioners can have his or her thoughts and movements read, unless they have moved beyond thoughts and fallen into the void.

BEGINNERS

When I teach, I do not wish to rob students of their natural movement. I wish to educate and open the movement of Aikido to them. Many beginners are taught a form which can take away their spontaneous movement. Then as they progress they learn techniques and pass through their grades to black belt and beyond. There comes a time when you have to junk all that you know, and then learn to move all over again. Not many people are prepared to do this after all that struggle, but it must be done to become free in movement. To flow as Aikido is intended, one must throw away the known and move into the unknown. I teach the energy of Aikido and the understanding of its movement. I never teach the beginner set beginner's practices. I start the beginner in where I am. Obviously I slow down for them and bring them on at their rate, but I do not drop my energy or the understanding. I teach at a high level of understanding, leaving everyone in a position to see and know what they are doing if they are able. Each sees and takes what one is able to, and one can only do this from one's own level. You can't see further than where you are.

I do not wish to remove one set of movements for another set of movements. I wish to wake every individual so that they begin to see by a process of real education, not just facts or technique cramming. Every movement is a fragment of energy. Eventually after long and deep training your energy begins to take shape. You see and understand a completing picture. You begin to move freely. You can feel your uke's energy and what that energy requires of you. I also believe that teaching this way keeps the beginner's interest and allows them to see into the distance without being cramped by a grading syllabus.

I do not allow fear on the mat. Never should fear arise in students, or if it does arise it must be recognised and helped away. A complete beginner may have some trepidation about starting but this should not turn to fear. It must be kind and friendly on the mat from the sensei down. I have seen fear on the mat. I have seen fear at courses which surface as judgements, unfriendliness and pain.

When beginners ask which foot to start with, I bring both their feet together into a normal standing posture. From this you can move anywhere. I leave them their feet and their movement. As they grow and understand they will know how to move their feet.

ATTACKS

Even though I do not teach Aikido as a martial art, I do teach it from receiving immediate energy, for example a fast close punch or strike. For this is where you start to learn about energy and movement. It is your conscious response that determines the rest of the move. That is if you get out of the way quickly enough to have a further response. It is fine to train with flowing techniques. They teach you how to move the hips and the rest of your body. But it is at the end of a fast punch or kick that your knowledge must be. Remember that a punch or kick is only dangerous for a very short distance. The rest is leading up to it and then past it. These are the areas you must recognise and move inside or outside of. These are your safe areas and your partner's vulnerability.

TRAILING ARM TECHNIQUE 1

Numbers 33 & 34 sequence of photographs demonstrate this movement beautifully. Notice the cut Yokomen Uchi and the trailing arm going to meet it. As the two meet and move round, you come through and turn to throw. The throw is your partner's momentum, and you feel it complete as you pass through. You do not disturb your partner's line, you just lend him your hand, the mirage of your body and step through and turn. Simple and so it should be. Please note that the movement takes place on the same spot. Here are four sequences of photographs, each revealing different aspects of the energy and care of these movements.

Trailing Arm Technique

1

2

3

4

5

Number 34

27

Trailing Arm Technique

Number 33

TRAILING ARM TECHNIQUE 1

As the cut comes you raise your arm to meet it, inside of wrist. There is no crash or Ki stop, just soft yielding contact. You allow your arm to be swept around by the cut. At the same time you move your body through and round your partner. As your body clears your partner's you throw. You do not interfere with your partner's direction. You leave him travelling in a straight line. You disappear. You must allow your arm to be free from the rest of your body as you move through. The throw is from the curve of your arm and the cutting edge of your hand (Tegatana) on to your partner's wrist. In each trailing arm technique, the trailing arm becomes the throwing arm. Numbers 3 and 4

Trailing Arm Technique

Number 3

Trailing Arm Technique

1

2

3

4

Photograph 2 demonstrates the body clearing passed the uke before the throw.

TRAILING ARM TECHNIQUES 2&3

Photograph sequences 14, 15, 16, 17, 18, 19, are trailing arm techniques from a punch to the face. Again the body moves leaving an arm floating against the blow. The other hand can be lifted to protect the face and act as a guide to the punch. Here you see moving inside then throwing outside, and moving outside and throwing inside. All these techniques have been photographed at full speed to give the correct flow and energy, consequently parts are missing.

Number 19 is a move outside and throw inside. Between the first two photographs a lot happens which is not shown, and that is the arm trailing and the body moving. It is the same with all the other shots. This is where you have to train to find the movement, remember the trailing arm is soft. The throw is the two arms curving together with the tegatana on the wrist. I have fitted some stills in, to show the parts of the missing movements.

Numbers 14, 18, 19 are outside, inside throws. also 26, 32, 36

Numbers 15, 16, 17 are inside, outside, this way has a fuller more rounded throw. also 29

Trailing Arm Technique 2 & 3

(a)

(b)

33

This is the beginning of inside outside trailing arm technique.

Photograph (a) shows the arm trailing against the punch arm as the body moves across. The other hand is acting as a guide and a protection against the punch.

Photograph (b) is the movement outside. It shows the two arms curved together with the tegatana on top in preparation for the throw. Between photograph (a) and (b) the punch is exhausted. The trailing arm takes the punch arm in a curve and then down into photograph (b) for the throw.

Trailing Arm Technique

Number 14

35

Trailing Arm Technique

Notice the harmony and softness of the throw in photograph 4 of number 14, and photograph 3 of number 18.

Number 18

Trailing Arm Technique 2 & 3

1(a)

1(b)

37

These photographs demonstrate the outside and then inside trailing arm technique. Which is the same theory as the inside outside movement, but in reverse. The difference between the two moves is the throw. Inside outside has a fuller throw.

Trailing Arm Technique

Number 16

Trailing Arm Technique

Number 17

Trailing Arm Technique

Photograph 2 shows the soft beginnings of the trailing arm.

Number 19

Trailing Arm Technique

Number 15

THE TRAILING ARM

With all trailing arm movements you move your trailing arm into the flow of the strike or punch. So that you flow out with the force of the strike, and then direct the movement. If you do not flow into the strike you will experience a block however light it is. It will not flow. The flowing in allows you to become one movement with your uke. From the moment you flow with your uke you are the centre. You do not take the centre, you become the centre. A great difference.

With all forms of attack you are training yourself to recognise the energy. Eventually you will be able to recognise the intention to strike, and how the strike will come before any physical manifestation appears.

The reason there are several sequences of the same technique is to give the feel of the movements. Each sequence reveals something about the movement. The same situation as when you are watching a demonstration during a training session.

Trailing Arm Technique

Number 26

Trailing Arm Technique

Number 29

Trailing Arm Technique

Notice the curving arms of the throw meeting in photograph 2 of both sequences.

Trailing Arm Technique

Number 36

TRAILING ARM 4

Your uke punches straight to your nose. Your hand meets the punch on the outside of the wrist as you drop your body below it. Allow your arm to blend as it meets the punch, and allow it to follow the punch energy as you drop and pass your body in front of your uke. As your body clears your uke, you take charge of the punch arm and throw. Notice how far the body drops to be completely away from the punch. It is a soundless meeting of hand to wrist.

Trailing Arm Technique

1

2

3

4

5

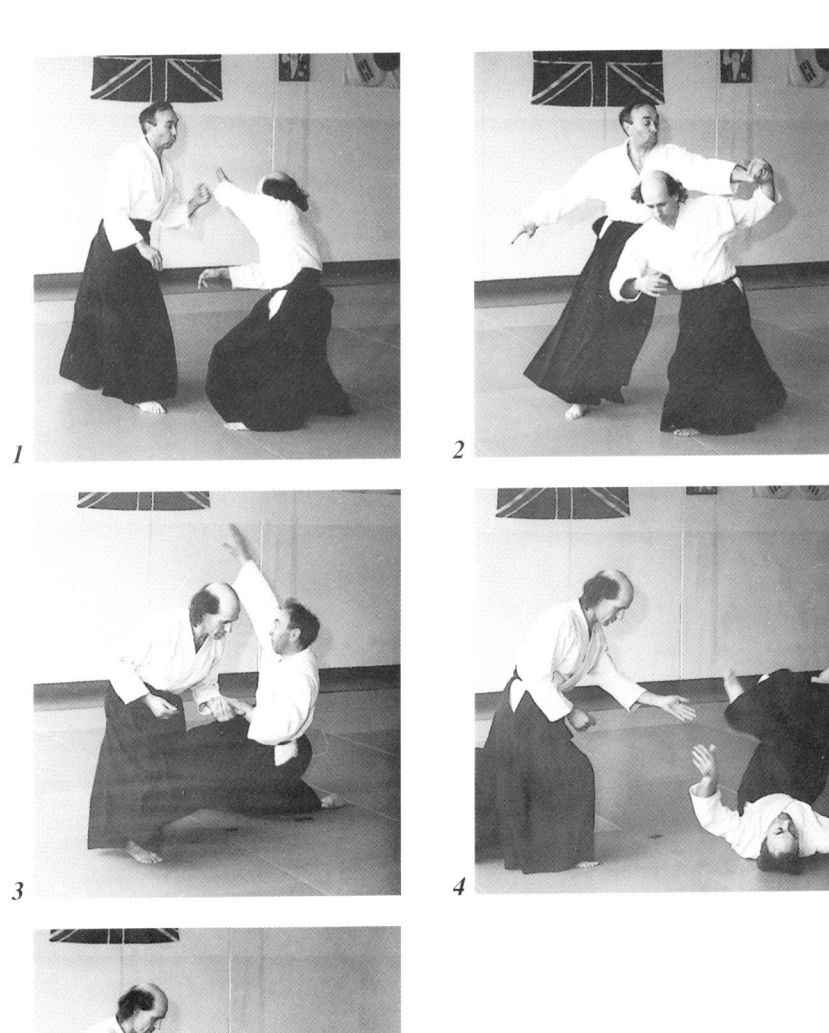

Number 27

TRAILING ARM TECHNIQUES 5 & 6

Uke attacks with a Shomen-Uchi cut. There are two approaches, but both have the same principle. The first approach is as your uke lifts for Shomen cut, that you allow your hand to flow up underneath it and then down underneath it. As the cut almost reaches its end, curve it back and round turning it into Ikkyo, numbers 5, 6, 7.

The second approach is to again follow the cut up but with the other hand. This time you take it straight back in a curve. So that your uke goes straight back. Numbers 20, 21. Here you are learning to flow with your partner's energy and blend with his Ki. Practice the silent soft meeting, and feel the strength of it.

Trailing Arm Technique

1

2

3

4

5

Number 7

Trailing Arm Technique   *Number 5*

Trailing Arm Technique

Number 6

Trailing Arm Technique

1

2

3

4

5

6

Number 20

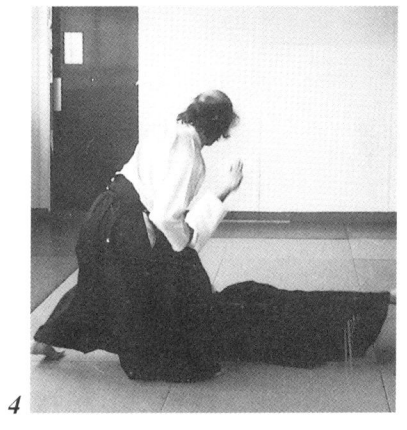

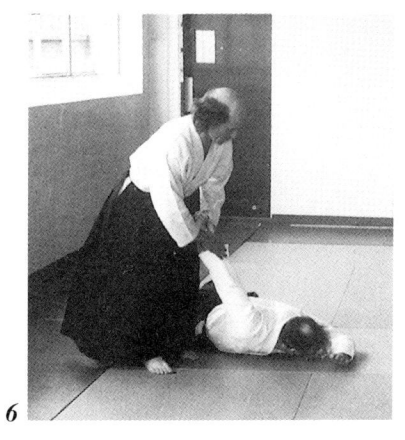

Trailing Arm Technique

Number 21

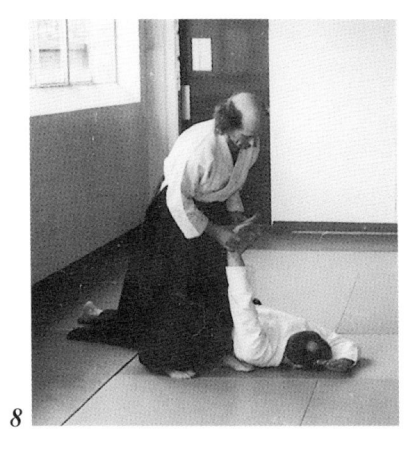

Trailing Arm Technique

The first photograph shows the flowing up and in. The second photograph shows the flowing out and becoming the centre.

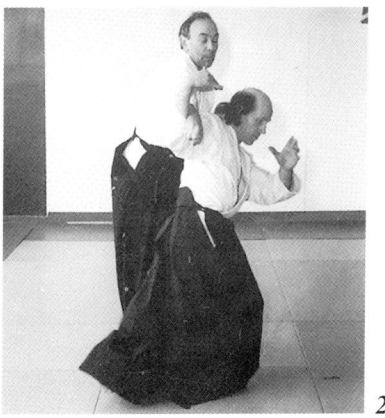

TRAILING ARM TECHNIQUE 7

Reverse Yokomen-Uchi cut. Allow the meeting arm to trail while moving the rest of you underneath. When underneath and the cut is nearly exhausted, you take the arm and sweep it through, a very powerful movement here. Then finish with a throw and arm lock.

Two beginnings

57

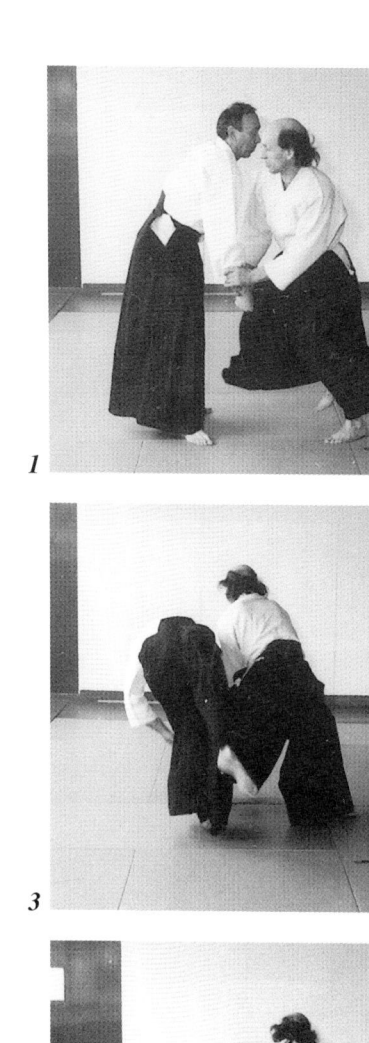

Trailing Arm Technique 7

Trailing Arm Technique

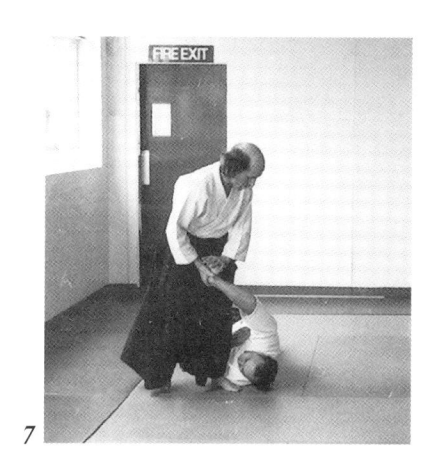

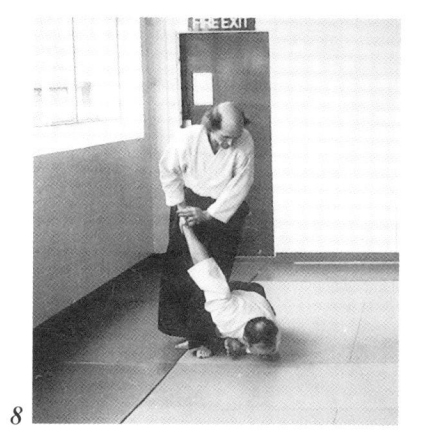

Between photographs 2 and 3 there is a very fast reverse turn.

TRAILING ARM TECHNIQUE 7

2(a)

2(b)

These stills show the trailing arm from reverse Yokomen-Uchi. You allow the meeting arm to trail as your body goes through after that you turn right round taking your uke with you and throw. It is a very fast turn. From still 3 you cut your partner's arm down in a curve between both your bodies turning you both the other way. Photograph 3 of number 24 follows on from still 3.

2(c)

Techa Nage

I have included Techa Nage because I like what is in it. Numbers 12, 13, 28. Techa Nage, heaven and earth throw. This is a blending of Ki and energy, they all are, but this one is an obvious one. This movement splits your partners Ki as you divide your hands, that is where the spark is. This one is from a straight punch number 28, from a Shomen-Uchi numbers 12, 13. For both you move aside with both hands above the punch or cut arm. One hand cuts the punch in a deep powerful sweeping circle, which turns the body taking it to earth. The other open hand takes the head by the chin if contact is made, often it is never made, and through, heaven. Techga Nage movement is the tearing of your partners Ki. To practice so that you understand this, stand still with your partner holding your wrists. Without any indication move with your whole body one hand to heaven and one to earth. If you are moving correctly, your partner will experience the tear all the way down the centre of the body. For it is powerful and does tear your partner's Ki, but not irreparably. This type of movement is the most violent movement you should ever make in Aikido.

Numbers 8, 9. Here you move just before your uke grasps your wrists. You split his Ki and send him to the ground. Your uke must be giving the correct energy for this movement to happen. You must suddenly at the right moment explode with energy, which will knock your partner back splitting his Ki.

Techa Nage

Number 12

Techa Nage

1

2

3

4

Number 13

64

Techa Nage

Photograph 2 is where the Ki is about to be unleashed.

Number 8

65

Techa Nage

Number 9

Techa Nage

Notice the solid rooted posture after throwing, in the last two photographs.

Number 31

Techa Nage

1

2

3

4

Number 28

Techa Nage

Notice in the first photograph that even though the punch is being thrown, that very little movement occurs until photograph 2. Try not to move too early and keep the gap between you narrow.

Number 35

USING TEGATANA

Do not move in a straight hard line with this technique. Numbers 10, 11, 30, 38. Your uke takes both your wrists. You absorb your uke's energy by moving backwards, number 38 shows this. You cut with the edge of the hands (tegatana) on the outside of your uke's wrists.

Using Tegatana

1

2

3

4

Number 10

70

One hand cuts through across the body to turn your uke, but remember all movements curve. You throw by turning your shoulder against your uke's other forearm and spinning him around your body and down. Turn him over and put on an arm lock. The arm that turns your uke's body curves and follows the throw.

Using Tegatana

5

6

7

8

Number 10

Using Tegatana

Number 11

Using Tegatana

5

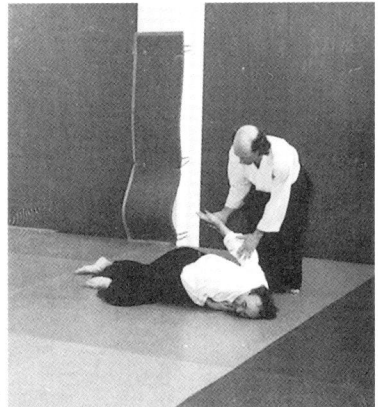

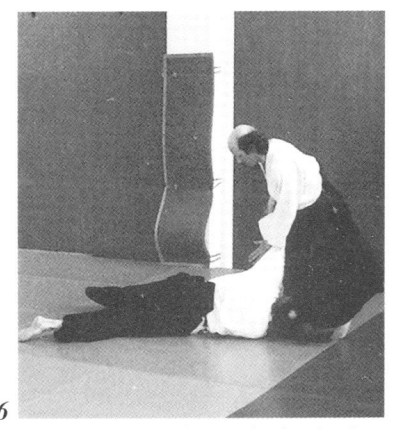

6

Photograph 3 shows the beginning of the throw with the shoulder against the uke's forearm. The cutting arm is curved in the direction of the thrust. Photograph 4 shows uke falling away from shoulder throw.

7

Number 11

73

Using Tegatana

1

2

3

4

Number 30

Using Tegatana

5

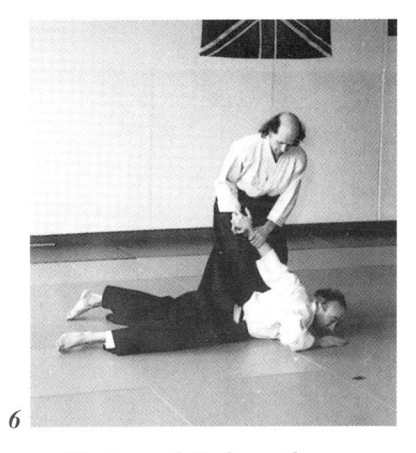

6

Photograph 2 shows the arm cutting across the uke's front. Remember that this is a curving cut and not a straight one.

7

Number 30

Using Tegatana

1

2

3

4

Number 38

Using Tegatana

5

6

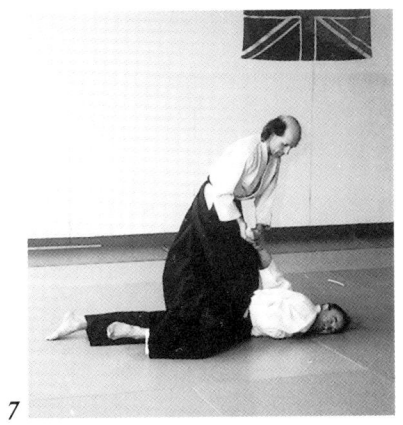

7

8

Number 38

TEGATANA

3(a) 3(b)

This group of four photographs demonstrates a throw by cutting with the tegatana into the palm of your uke's hand. It is a pleasant technique to fall from. Do not put Nikkyo on your uke's wrist with the supporting hand as you cut. For it does not allow the throw, it just takes the uke straight down. A simple movement. Bring both tegatana to the outside of your uke's wrists, causing his wrists to be back to back. You select one wrist to hold and throw into its palm with the tegatana of the other hand.

3(c)

3(d)

USING FINGER AND THUMB

This movement is using the open vee of finger and thumb to throw your uke. Numbers 1, 2, 37. Here your uke grabs both of your wrists. You drop back absorbing his energy and feeling for his centre and Ki. You rotate your wrists so that you hold your uke's wrists from underneath by the vee of finger and thumb. At the same time you turn the back of his wrists to face each other. One arm drops across your uke's front in a powerful curve. The other arm you lift up and pass underneath .The vee of finger and thumb rotates completely around this wrist, and as you clear your partner's body you throw to his centre. Remember to pass as close as possible underneath the armpit. This is the highest point for your head and away from dropping elbows. You take your partner's centre and Ki immediately you drop back. This should be the way with all Aikido movement. Once you move in the flow of your uke you are leading the movement.

1 *2* *3* *4* *5* *6*

Notice the absorption of the uke's energy in the first photograph.

Number 37

*Watch the elbows in this one in photograph 2.
It is easy to get them too high.*

Number 1

1 *2*

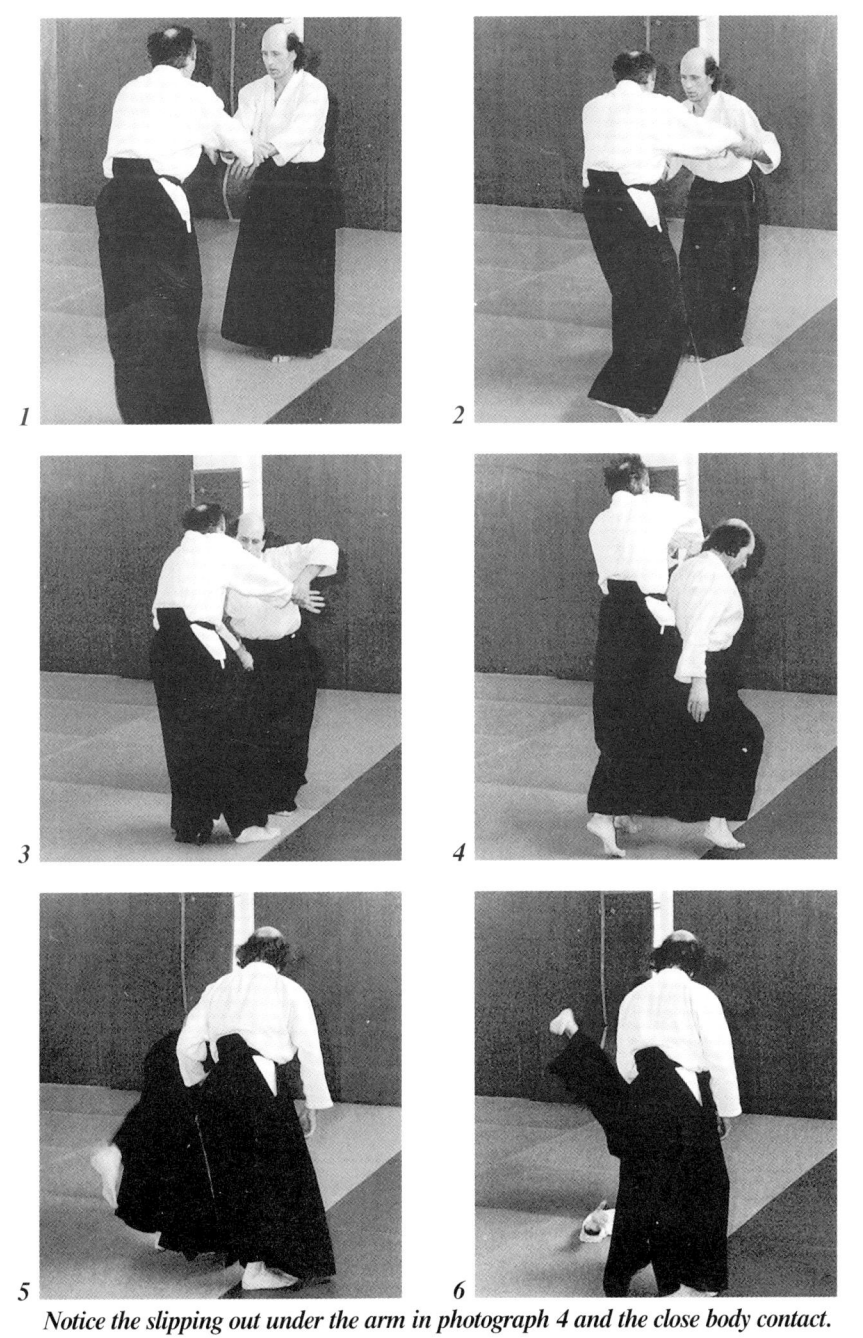

3 *4*

5 *6*

N
u
m
b
e
r

2

Notice the slipping out under the arm in photograph 4 and the close body contact.

83

USE OF KI

4(a) *4(b)*

Use Ki kicks and punches. These four photographs demonstrate the use of Ki from a kick. The punch or kick does not contact, it delivers Ki. It retracts the energy back into your partner. Notice in 4(a) the way my uke is up on his toes in response to the Ki kick to his throat. When using Ki kicks keep the body forward. Remember centre and sixty per cent body weight forward, and kick like that. In 4(b) the Yokomen-Uchi attack is

USE OF KI

4(c) *4(d)*

caught under the armpit in a wrist lock. Notice that my uke is still on his toes. In 4(c) at the top of the arm onto the shoulder there is a little muscle. Beyond it is a pressure point into which you place two finger tips and direct your uke to third point. Also the tegatana of the holding arm cuts onto the uke's wrist as you throw him. 4(d) shows the uke having fallen, with the wrist lock still applied.

CONCLUSION

Aikido like many other martial arts has been institutionalised and strangled by the grading system. A grading system produces acquisition and possession. It has no feel for heart or flow and the living movement. It is dead, but unfortunately very alive. To grow you have to pass beyond the grading structure to discover the heart, and surrender yourself completely to your chosen discipline. This takes some doing. Traditionally one stayed with a teacher until he could teach you no more and you moved on. Or he would tell you to move on and present you with a scroll. Or you might just stay with him until you could see enough of the universe and realise what you were doing and why, and what you were going to do about it. The training is spiritual and must be to have any worth. Without it, it is empty, useless. It is about growth of the being which is covered in a thick layer of ego, the ideas about what you think you are. Now a grading system just adds another layer of ego. They also preserve a hierarchy and a solid wall against anything different.

There is a system, yet no system. It will appear a system but it isn't if the sensei is free. All systems shackle and imprison one. If you look there are many seemingly contradictory statements, but these contradictions are truths. You will come to understand these, not with your mind, but with your heart.

It is difficult to write much about the movements I have shown. For they need to be taught live, where I can watch and feel each person's energy blocks and flow. For when I teach there are many nuances necessary, which are not possible to put into a book.

I concentrate on the opening punch, strike or kick energy. If this area is not understood and mastered there is no throw or arm lock. Therefore this is the beginning of understanding the essence and energy of Aikido. For the very first step is to move out of the way, away from the punch or kick. While you are avoiding the blow there is no thought of injuring anybody or subjugating them. Now this first state is where you must remain, you should be lost in the immediacy of the movement all the way through. From getting out of the way, to the throw and or arm lock. Within that first movement there is no time for mind, no time for fear, hate or anger. Just getting out of the way is all that is conscious, the mind has not yet formulated any ideas or set responses. This is why you move quickly.

In Aikido you must learn to move without the mind. You must feel the movements with your entire being. You must engulf the punch or kick with your entire being. You must be conscious of all energy, but with an intelligence that is not the mind. The mind hinders, it grabs hold of techniques, names, grading syllabus all the ritual reasons. It goes on and on taking you nowhere apart from the mind, and the world of the mind. Where everyone asks you, "What grade are you?" Forget it. Discover the energy instead, then you can perhaps begin to really move. To follow this course you must dare to be different, following where your heart leads and not your head.

The big question to ask your self is WHY? Why am I doing it. Is it to learn something separate from me. Or is it to learn something that will become part of me and cause me to grow. If it does not cause your mind problems and force you to grow in awareness, then the training is worthless.